THE KAIZEN FREEWAY

A high speed route to process improvement

Ross A Petermann

THE KAIZEN FREEWAY

Copyright ©2011 by Ross A. Petermann

This book is dedicated to all of the people who strive every day to improve their businesses in ways that not only helps their bottom line but also enhances the workplace and the lives of those who work there. Driving improvements is both challenging and enriching and I encourage you to involve as many people as you can in the improvement process. With more people engaged, not only will the solutions be better but they will be much more likely to be sustained. I am confident that once people learn the Kaizen Freeway techniques that the improvement efforts will grow exponentially and your business or organization will see positive results that would have seemed impossible before.

Ross A. Petermann

All rights reserved. No part of this book may be reproduced by any photographic, mechanical or electronic process or stored in a retrieval system, transmitted, or otherwise be copied for public or private use without prior written permission from the author.

ISBN-10: 1493582720
ISBN 13: 9781493582723
Library of Congress Control Number: 2013922113
CreateSpace Independent Publishing Platform,
North Charleston, South Carolina

THE KAIZEN FREEWAY

A high speed route to process improvement

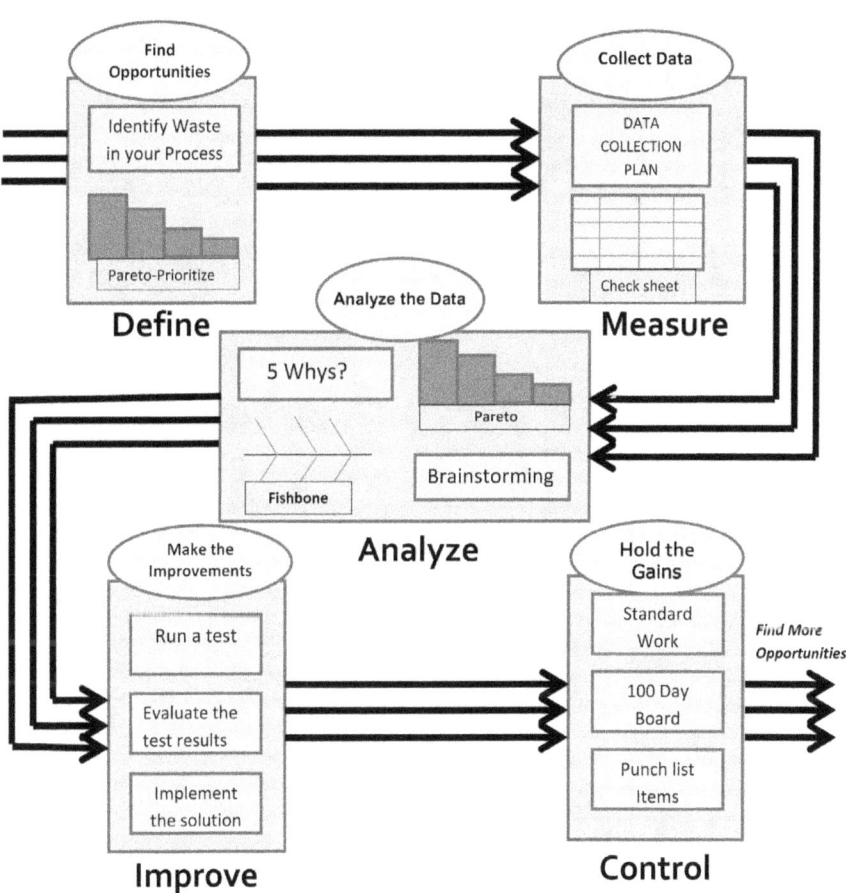

TABLE OF CONTENTS

		Page
1	Kaizen Roadmap	1
2	What is a kaizen?	3
3	What is the purpose of a kaizen?	5
4	Kaizen key steps	7
5	Managing team dynamics	17
6	Kaizen preparation checklist	21
7	Typical kaizen agenda	23
8	Kaizen leader characteristics	25
9	Kaizen leader responsibilities	27
10	Kaizen leader tips	29
11	Kaizen ground rules	31
12.	Summary	33
	Toolkit	35
	a. Lean building blocks	35
	b. Process map	36
	c. Visual Controls	36
	d. 8 Wastes	36
	e. 5S	37
	f. 5 W's and 1 H	37
	g. Data Collection Plan	38
	h. Check Sheet Example	39
	i. 5 Why's	41
	j. Brainstorming	44
	k. Fishbone Diagram	45

l.	Pareto Diagram	46
m.	Planning a meeting	47

Glossary · · · 49

References · · · 51

INTRODUCTION

A key element of continuous improvement efforts is the ability to identify and eliminate waste and drive performance improvement in day to day operations. The many small (and not so small) improvements that are made every day ensure that a business stays ahead of the competition and relevant in an ever changing world.

One effective way of quickly improving performance is through kaizens. Kaizens are a key element in LEAN, the managing process developed by Toyota (see LEAN Building Blocks in the **Toolkit**). Kaizens are focused, short term, team-based improvement efforts that can be as short as an hour or last for several days. Short kaizens are sometimes called "point kaizens".

Kaizens or kaizen events have improved operations in hundreds of businesses and manufacturing operations. Kaizens can improve safety, quality, productivity and the work environment...both manufacturing and business processes. They can be used for any kind of process improvement effort – both physical and transactional. Kaizens are focused efforts that deliver results – fast! They can be used to tackle chronic problems or ones that have just appeared. Another important benefit is that those on the kaizen team have fun working together and feel good about seeing the fruits of their labor. They build teamwork and help create the involvement culture that can be leveraged for future improvement efforts.

In addition to getting quick results, it is critical to sustain the improvements made during the kaizen. Codifying the changes into "standard work" or "operating directions" will help to ensure that the changes are maintained by the organization.

This book provides details of how to design, organize and run a kaizen event. It also provides a high level overview of several tools (**Toolkit**) that can be used by the kaizen team to identify opportunities, analyze data and determine the best solution to improve the process. The "Kaizen Freeway" is built around the five steps, DMAIC (Define, Measure, Analyze, Improve and Control), used in Six Sigma. These steps ensure that the kaizen, just like a Six Sigma project, covers all the key aspects needed for a successful improvement effort.

The keys for a successful kaizen are good planning, strong leadership and empowering the people who know the most about the problem to figure out the best solution. They will have fun doing it and it will open the door to future opportunities.

Ross A. Petermann

1.
KAIZEN ROADMAP

The following are the major steps for ensuring an effective kaizen. Not all kaizens will use each step in depth, but it is a good idea to consider each step to make sure that no important aspect is overlooked.

Pre Kaizen Preparations
1. FIND OPPORTUNITIES
   a. Select a key issue or waste in your area
   b. Develop a charter for the kaizen
   c. Choose your team

Kaizen Event
2. COLLECT DATA
3. ANALYZE the DATA
4. MAKE the IMPROVEMENTS
   a. Test the possible solutions
   b. Analyze the test results
   c. Choose the best solution
   d. Implement the solution
5. SUSTAIN the GAINS
   a. Develop a control plan
   b. Incorporate changes into "standard work"

Post Kaizen
6. PRESENT the RESULTS
7. RECOGNIZE the TEAM
8. COMPLETE any PUNCHLIST ITEMS

2.
WHAT IS A KAIZEN?

- A kaizen is a small group of employees voluntarily working together to solve problems or make improvement in their work area.
- Kaizen events tap into the collective knowledge of the people closest to the problem and those most impacted by the results.
- Team size can vary but normally is 3-10 people. The number of people depends on the scope of the kaizen. Too few people can negatively impact the quality of the results. Too many can make management of the event difficult or limit participation. If the work can be easily divided into sub teams, more team members can be accommodated.
- Team members usually come from the area impacted by the kaizen but can include others that may bring knowledge to the kaizen subject matter. Generally, it is best to include different functions and have both new people to the area and those with more experience. Customers of the process can also be incorporated into the event when appropriate.
- Kaizens are organized events but depend on the creativity, ideas and flexibility of the team.
- Kaizens can use a variety of tools and approaches. The tools that are used need to be tailored to the problem being addressed. For example, the use of 5 Why's (**Toolkit**) is an excellent technique for driving to the root cause of a problem.

- Generally, organizations new to kaizen events will begin by addressing a more straightforward problem, with limited scope or choose a 5S (**Toolkit**) event to learn the kaizen way of improvement.
- Subjects that are particularly controversial such as those impacting roles, reducing headcount or impacting pay are generally not suitable for a kaizen event.

3.
WHAT IS THE PURPOSE OF A KAIZEN?

- Kaizen events are aimed at delivering specific, measureable improvements in a short period of time and helping to create an environment of continuous improvement.
- Kaizen events can address a wide range of problems or redesign processes to improve efficiency, quality or morale.
- The problem area can be a recent event or can be one that has been a chronic problem in the plant or business.
- Another source of ideas for kaizens comes from the identification of one of the 8 Wastes in LEAN. (**Toolkit**)
- Ideally, topics for a kaizen should be both important to the business and important to the people in the kaizen event.
- Most improvements are completed during the kaizen event or immediately afterward. Sometimes there are additional punchlist items put on a "30 Day List" but every effort should be made to complete items during the kaizen.
- Some kaizens require more than one event in which the first event begins the analysis and the follow-up event completes the work.

4.
KAIZEN KEY STEPS

STEP 1. FIND OPPORTUNITIES
A. Select a key issue or waste in your area

There are usually a number of problem areas or improvement opportunities in any process so it should not be difficult to find something to address in a kaizen. One approach is to identify one of the 8 Wastes (**Toolbox**) which is one of the key improvement tools in LEAN (see Lean Building Blocks in the **Toolbox**). As the area gets better at identifying "waste", the challenge will be deciding which opportunity to address first. Here are the 8 Wastes:

1. Defects in quality
2. Over production – more than is needed by the customer
3. Waiting
4. Not Engaging Employees
5. Transportation
6. Inventory/Storage
7. Motion
8. Excess Processing

Keep in mind that "waste" is usually a result of a poor process or confusion over how the process is to work...not due to people's performance.

As you first start with kaizens, it is best to choose problems that have a good likelihood of a successful outcome. More difficult or complex problems can certainly be addressed by kaizens but should be done once the organization has had some kaizen experience.

B. Develop a charter

A charter (see example in Figure 1 below) is a critical first step in defining what a kaizen event will address and who will be on the team. The charter defines the scope of the problem to be addressed and the goal for the kaizen event. A simple process map (**Toolkit**) is very useful in clarifying the scope. The process map defines the inputs, process steps and outputs of the process to be addressed in the kaizen and should be used to introduce the kaizen team to the scope on the first day. The process owner should sign off on the charter to ensure that he/she is in support of the upcoming event and agrees with the process map.

For larger events, area leadership normally will be present at the kick-off meeting and the closing presentation. It is important to confirm this with the leadership well in advance of the event. In some cases, leadership and/or process owners may want a short debrief meeting at the end of each day of the event. For point kaizens, a quick report to the process owner at the end of the kaizen event is normally all that is required.

A well designed agenda is also critical to the success of a kaizen. The **Toolkit** provides a simple meeting design (Planning a Meeting) process to help in developing a daily agenda. It is important to revisit the agenda at the end of each day to make adjustments based on the progress that day.

FIGURE 1. COMPONENTS OF A KAIZEN CHARTER

- What is the problem/waste to be addressed?
- What is the scope?
- What are the objectives?
- What are the potential benefits?
- What resources may be required?
- Who is the process owner?
- When will it happen?
- Who is on the team/ Who is the team leader?

C. Select Team Members

Team membership is critical to the success of a kaizen. The team should be determined after the scope and objectives in the charter are defined. With the charter in place, it is easier to identify the skills needed for success and that will lead to selection of the best team members.

The kaizen leader is particularly critical since he/she will set the tone for the event and work toward a solution while ensuring good team involvement. As the use of kaizens expands in your organization, it is important to develop new leaders. One way of doing this is to provide leadership opportunities such as leading kaizen sub teams or assisting the leader in planning the kaizen. This will build their confidence and allow observation of their leadership skills. See **7. Kaizen Leader Characteristics** to aid in the selection process.

A point kaizen that may only last a few hours can be comprised of a 2-3 person team. Longer events with a more complicated scope require more thoughtful membership consideration. For key members, the kaizen schedule may have to be adjusted to ensure that they are available.

Team members are expected to be available 100% of the time. Experience shows that "part time" members are problematic since their time commitment to the event is unclear. The only exception can be "consultants" who are asked to be available to supply expertise at specific times during the event. It is best to anticipate when they will be needed and get it on their schedules.

For more information on managing the team process, see **5. Managing Team Dynamics.**

STEP 2. COLLECT DATA

Data and information are important inputs to ensure that the team is able to make data-driven decisions. Without data, the team may resort to opinions that lead to poor decisions. Without data, team decisions may be driven more by powerful personalities and not by the integrated consensus of the all the team members.

Data also helps link a cause and effect and aides the team at getting to a true root cause of the problem. The team should avoid jumping to a solution too quickly. They should "let the data speak" and then build a consensus based on what it tells the team.

Determining what data should be collected depends on the problem. Hopefully, the item(s) being improved can be measured. These are called "Y" in Six Sigma. Without a measurement of "Y", it will be difficult to determine if an improvement has been accomplished by the kaizen.

For simple kaizens or 5S events, data collection should be very easy or not be required, but it is always good to see what data is available and determine if there is a way to measure the improvements that will be made in the kaizen.

Often it is better to collect data before the kaizen event using a Data Collection Plan. (**Toolkit**). The Data Collection Plan considers the amount of data, the time window for collection, how the data will be captured and who will do it.

Ideally, data should be from the recent past to ensure a clear picture of the current state. If there is not enough data, it may be best to delay the kaizen until enough data is collected. It is also important to make sure that the measurement system is accurate so that when improvements are made, the organization can be confident that the improvements are real. Also, it is best to capture enough data over a time period that reflects the true process and not some short term variation.

STEP 3. ANALYZE THE DATA

When enough accurate data has been gathered, the next step is to analyze it to try and determine the possible causes of the problem. Some data analysis techniques are shown in the **Toolkit**.

This analysis can be done before or during the event. If it is done before the event, it is important to review the data analysis with the team at the start of the event to build understanding and consensus about what it says.

STEP 4. MAKE THE IMPROVEMENTS

When the team has analyzed the data, the next step is to develop some theories of what might be causing the problem or how best to eliminate it. These can be generated in brainstorming sessions (**Toolkit**). The challenge is to determine one or more countermeasures that the team feels is the best way to reduce or prevent recurrence of the problem or improve the process. Ideally, the proposed solution(s) is not expensive or time consuming to implement.

A. Test the Possible Solutions

Once one or more possible solutions or countermeasures have been developed, it is time to evaluate them in the real world. Sometimes, this can be done very easily by the team running simple tests of the proposed changes. The team should carefully define the changes and ensure that those carrying out the tests are clear on what is to be done. If there is data to be gathered during the test, the plan should include a Data Collection Plan.

If the change has any safety or quality risk, the proposed change must be reviewed carefully with process experts. In these cases, a test will likely require an authorized Test Authorization or similar document.

B. Analyze the results and choose a final solution

The team should analyze the test results and decide on the best solution. Often minor adjustments will need to be made based on the learnings from the test. If the changes are significant, a second test may be necessary. The key is to make sure that the proposed solution makes the improvement that is needed and that it can be sustained by the organization.

C. Implement the solution

The most exciting part of a kaizen is the actual implementation which may include physical changes or only be procedural. In any event, it is best to implement all the changes possible during the event. Implementation may also include training, changes to existing procedures or development of new procedures.

STEP 5. HOLD THE GAINS
The next step is to make sure that there is adequate understanding, training and procedures in place to sustain the new improvements. This is called a "control plan" which defines everything required to institutionalize the change. The procedures must address what is to be done, when it is to be done and who is responsible. Ideally, this is accomplished by changing operating directions or maintenance procedures.

The aim is to ensure the changes are incorporated in the organization's "standard work".

Another tool for sustaining the gains is the use of visual management (**Toolkit**). Visual management provides visual information to allow for proper operation or to alert workers of unusual conditions. These can include short printed instructions, status lights, photos of standard conditions or any other visual reminders that help sustain the new procedures or standards developed in the kaizen.

Some organizations use a "100 Day Board" to track whether the changes are being maintained. Someone in leadership or from the kaizen team monitors the changes periodically and if the changes are still in place, the count of days continues. If, on the other hand, the process has broken down, the day counter is reset to zero. Only after 100 consecutive days, should the changes be viewed as "permanent" by the organization. Ideally, further auditing should be done after six months or a year to ensure the changes are being maintained.

STEP 6. PRESENT THE RESULTS

At the conclusion of the event, it is important to review the findings with the process owner and area leadership. For some small kaizens, this is done informally in the area. For larger events, a formal presentation can be done by the team members. This communication is important as it informs the process owner of the planned changes and clarifies the organization's new responsibilities.

STEP 7. RECOGNIZE THE TEAM

Also, at this time, the leadership should thank the team for their efforts and their accomplishments. In larger events, some form of recognition may be given to team members such as a lunch or small gift. If the kaizen savings are significant, organizations may consider monetary awards. Such awards can be problematic by causing conflict or jealousy. They also can establish a precedent making recognition in future kaizens more difficult. Thoughtful consideration should be given to any such award and ideally be given in the context of a well-defined, consistent award system.

STEP 8. COMPLETE ANY PUNCHLIST ITEMS

Any remaining items from the kaizen that were not completed need to be completed in a timely fashion…ideally in 30 days. Experience has shown that these items can "get lost" if not completed promptly. Normally, the kaizen leader working with the process owner has responsibility to see that the items are completed.

5.
MANAGING TEAM DYNAMICS

To achieve optimum results from your kaizen, it is essential to manage the team dynamics. It is a challenge to get a diverse group of people, who may not have worked together before, organized into a team and working toward a common goal. This is particularly difficult with the relatively short length of a kaizen event.

A key first step is to get everyone to know each other. One effective technique is to pair off team members and have them introduce each other. Ideally, people should be paired with someone they don't know. The introduction can include their name, current job, work history, hobbies and perhaps something unusual about them.

Another key is to have the team establish a set of mutually agreed upon ground rules. An example list is shown in Chapter 11 but it is best to have the team define their own set. The ground rules can be used during the kaizen if team members violate them to a point that impacts the team's progress. Also, for an extended kaizen, a quick review of the ground rules each morning is recommended.

Meeting room set-up is also important. It is best to set up tables in a "U shape" so that everyone can see and hear each other. Choose a room so that people don't feel cramped. Since participants may not be used to sitting for long periods, provide frequent short breaks but set a time so breaks don't get overextended.

Another way to help create a relaxed environment is an icebreaker called "two truths and a lie". In this activity, each person writes down two things that are true about themselves and one that is a lie. The leader gathers the sheets and then reads them to the team. The challenge is to identify who wrote it and which of the three statements is the lie. These can be reviewed all at once or a few done periodically during the day. This activity provides an opportunity to learn more about each person and their choice of "the lie" can also provide insight into their personalities.

Another challenge for the kaizen leader is to monitor team participation. Two situations in particular need to be in focus: dominance and non-participation. Naturally, some people on the team will be more talkative and outgoing while others will tend to be quiet and listen. The challenge for the leader is to ensure that one or two people don't take over the kaizen and their ideas dominate the discussion and the outcome. The power in a kaizen is the joining of the diverse ideas from all the team members so dominance by one or two people can destroy that process.

The first step is to recognize that it is happening by observing body language of people who are not as naturally outgoing. If they are not engaged, it may be that they are feeling dominated by one or two people who are doing all the talking. If this is happening, the first step is to directly ask for their ideas on the subject being discussed. Another technique is to capture ideas on a chart pad from each of the team members in turn. That provides balance to the input and demonstrates that everyone's ideas are important. Another approach is to break the team into smaller groups where it is more likely that the quieter people will feel more comfortable talking.

If the problem becomes acute, it may be necessary for the kaizen leader to talk privately with the person who is dominating the event. This step should only be taken if their behavior is resulting in a significant breakdown of the team dynamics. Hopefully, the person will receive the input positively and continue to be engaged but in a more balanced manner.

Another challenge can occur if a team member wants to discuss concerns outside the scope of the kaizen. This is not unusual and the kaizen leader's response should be to simply restate their concern. Once the concern is fully understood, the leader should ask the team whether they feel it is in scope or rather should it be placed on the "parking lot". The "parking lot" is used to capture any ideas or concerns outside of scope and then are assigned to someone to address outside the kaizen. A courtesy to the person raising the concern is to get their concurrence when putting the item on the "parking lot".

One additional way to gain insight into how the team is functioning is to ask for "pluses and opportunities" at the end of each day. Ask team members to write on a "sticky note" the aspects of the kaizen that are going well and on a separate note concerns or ideas on what could be done better. They then place them on a chart pad with the two categories. The next morning, the kaizen leader can review the input with the team. Any personal or sensitive items should be removed from the board and handled privately.

6.
KAIZEN PREPARATION CHECKLIST

1. Charter complete and approved by process owner
2. Date and time are set
3. Members selected, informed, available and committed
4. Team leader identified and committed
5. Data gathered and analyzed
6. Rooms and meals scheduled
7. Paper, pencils, tape, computer projectors, easels, etc. prepared
8. Detailed agenda planned for the entire event
9. Any sub teams and their leaders identified
10. Recognition awards in hand
11. Any other support personnel (i.e. part time consultant) are on board
12. 100 Day Board in hand
13. Closing presentation scheduled and leadership informed

7.
TYPICAL KAIZEN AGENDA

- **Safety Message**
- **Welcome**
- **Icebreaker**
- **Ground Rules**
- **Charter Review**
  - Review Charter in detail — Gain support by the team
- **Problem review**
  - Include pre kaizen data analysis – agree on how to measure success
  - Get input from the team members
- **Plant tour**
- **Training**
  - Train on material important to the particular kaizen
- **Data Analysis and Discussion**
- **Use tools to generate possible solutions**
  - Brainstorming, Fishbone Diagram, 5 Why
- **Converge on possible solution(s)**
- **Test solution(s)**
- **Evaluate the results**
- **Decide on the best solution**
- **Make the changes including documentation**
- **Define control plans to ensure sustainability**
- **Report out to leadership**
- **Recognize the team**

8.
KAIZEN LEADER CHARACTERISTICS

- Prior experience in team leadership
- Good planner
- Familiar with the Kaizen Freeway
- Guides – not directs
- Good listener
- Avoids providing answers
- Encourages participation by everyone
- Able to address behavior issues
- Flexible but results oriented
- Able to readjust the schedule if circumstances dictate
- Good at aligning team members skills and interests with the work to be done

9. KAIZEN LEADER RESPONSIBILITIES

1. Help develop the charter and ensure alignment with the process owner
2. Along with area leadership, identify and recruit team members
3. Plan the kaizen event details (timing, room locations, agenda, meals, etc.)
4. Identify the data needed and initiate any required data collection
5. Manage the event:
    a. Ensure everyone is participating
    b. Make sure the team uses the data
    c. Work toward consensus
    d. Ensure the team stays on task and schedule
6. Help the team use the right tools
7. Keep leadership/process owner informed of progress and aware of any issues
8. Help the team analyze the data and develop proposed solutions
9. Ensure tests are planned and executed
10. Help team plan and deliver results presentation
11. Recognize the team members
12. Follow up on any punch list items

10. KAIZEN LEADER TIPS

- Make sure leadership is fully on board with the charter in the beginning
- Be absolutely clear on what is in scope and what is out – avoid "Scope Creep"
- Start on time – End on time
- Don't make the days too long
- Address problems quickly – personal conflict, attendance, group dominance
- Make sure everyone's opinions are heard – don't let one or two people dominate
- Get people out of the conference room in the first two hours – it is critical for the team to observe the subject of the kaizen first hand
- Have an idea of possible solutions before the event starts – Only introduce if necessary
- Provide any basic training that is critical to the success of the kaizen in the first half day
- Encourage the use of data – not relying just on opinion
- Capture any ideas that are out of scope and provide to the process owner for future consideration
- Ask for "sticky note" reflections (both +'s and "opportunities") at the end of each day
- Debrief at the end of each day with the process owner and other interested leadership

11.
KAIZEN GROUND RULES

- No rank
- Work as a team
- Listen
- Be open minded
- Positive attitude
- Stay focused and on task
- Be open to change
- No blame
- Be on time
- Respect each other
- No "dumb" questions
- Test out new ideas
- Work hard
- Have fun!

12.
SUMMARY

The kaizen is a simple, yet powerful tool that can revolutionize your organization by engaging everyone in the improvement process. By harnessing the knowledge and experience of your employees, the opportunities to improve are unlimited.

The "Kaizen Freeway" is intended to mimic a kaizen: simple, practical and results oriented. By thoughtfully following the steps and guidelines, anyone should be able to design and carry out a successful event.

Like any significant organizational change, there will be skeptics and perhaps some bumps in the road. These should be expected and by learning from each event, successive kaizens will become easier. Experience will also allow you to take on more difficult and more impactful opportunities.

Start with an important but manageable issue. Carefully design the event, choose the right team and have fun carrying it out. It won't be long before others will have ideas for the next kaizen and want to take on leadership roles. Your business or organization will be pleased with the results and grateful that you introduced the power of kaizen!

TOOLKIT

a) Lean building blocks:

Continuous Improvement

Kanban/Pull Systems	KAIZENS	Asset Care
Visual Management	Root Cause Failure Analysis	Waste Identification and Elimination
Standard Work	Batch Size Reduction	Teamwork
Visual Controls	5s	Quality
Value Stream Mapping	Set up Time Reduction	Flow

b) Process Map:

Everything can be viewed as a process …a series of steps or activities that transform inputs into outputs that are of value to a customer.

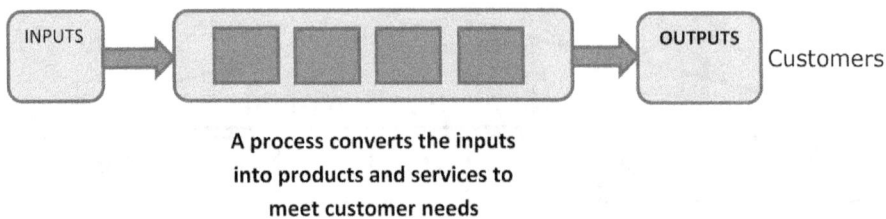

A process converts the inputs into products and services to meet customer needs

c) Visual Controls:

Simple visual signals or data that provide immediate understanding of a situation or condition and allow both shopfloor personnel and managers to monitor a process or alert them to hazards. These can include boards, signs, lines on the floor, lights, color coding and kanban cards.

d) 8 Wastes:

1. Defects in quality
2. Over production – more than the customer needs
3. Waiting
4. Not engaging employees
5. Transportation
6. Inventory/Storage
7. Motion
8. Excess Processing

e) 5S:

5S is not "super housekeeping"...it is a foundation for all improvement efforts

1. Sort – Identify what is needed and what is not
2. Shine – Clean and polish and eliminate contamination sources
3. Set in order – Keep all items in a specific, identified location
4. Standardize – Set standards for each area to remain clean and organized
5. Sustain – Put in place procedures and responsibilities to maintain the area

f) 5 W's and 1 H:

FOR PROBLEM OR IMPROVEMENT EFFORTS:
1. Who is involved/knowledgeable about the problem or situation?
2. What are the possible reasons or causes for what is happening?
3. When does it happen? When does it NOT happen?
4. Where does it happen?
5. Why? Why? Why? Why? Why? (5 Whys)
6. How could it happen?

FOR PLANNING ACTIVITIES:
1. Who is responsible?
2. What is to be done?
3. When will it be done? In what order will it be done?
4. Why are we doing it?
5. How will it be done?

g) Data Collection Plan:

Data Name	Time Window	Data Type	Data Source	# of Datapoints	Responsibility
Description of Data to be recorded	The period of time when the data was (or is) to be generated	Is the data the variable to be improved (Y) or is it one of the variables that may be controlled to make the improvement(X)?	Where is the data stored or where will it be captured?	How much data is to be captured?	Who is responsible for collecting the data?

h) Check Sheet Example:

Here is an example of using a check sheet method to investigate and develop ways to reduce customer complaints. Going through the last four years of complaints provides the following information. This list shows complaint number, manufacturing plant and the nature of the complaint.

Complaint #	Manf. Location	Type of Complaint
1	Plant 1	Shipping Error
2	Plant 2	Cut Quality
3	Plant 3	Contam-Metal
4	Plant 2	Contam-Metal
5	Plant 4	Melt Viscosity
6	Plant 3	Contam-Cross
7	Plant 2	Cut Quality
8	Plant 1	Contam-Cross
9	Plant 1	Contam-Metal
10	Plant 1	Melt Viscosity
11	Plant 1	Melt Viscosity
12	Plant 1	Melt Viscosity
13	Plant 4	Melt Viscosity
14	Plant 1	Contam-Cross
15	Plant 5	Contam-Cross
16	Plant 1	Melt Viscosity

A check sheet for complaint-by-type would look like the following. Getting more specific about the type of contamination involved in the complaints provides a better idea of what is causing customer problems that need to be addressed. It also might prevent addressing the "wrong" problem.

COMPLAINT BY TYPE

Type of Complaint	Number of Complaints	Total Number
Shipping Error	1	1
Cut Quality	11	2
Contam-Metal	111	3
Contam-Cross	1111	4
Melt Viscosity	111111	6

There is one more way to look at the data using check sheets that might provide even more information. A check sheet that lists complaint type down the left-hand side and the manufacturing plant across the top provides one sheet that gives all the information in the previous two tables. As a bonus, this format shows how many of each type of complaint was produced at each plant.

Complaint By Type	Plant 1	Plant 2	Plant 3	Plant 4	Plant 5	TOTAL
Shipping Error	1					1
Cut Quality		11				2
Contam-Metal	1	1	1			3
Contam-Cross	11		1		1	4
Melt Viscosity	1111			11		6
TOTAL	8	3	2	2	1	16

i) 5 Whys:

The "5 Why" analysis is a simple yet powerful problem solving tool that helps determine the root cause of a problem. Many times people tend to stop looking after only the immediate cause of a problem is determined. This methodology helps teams look beyond the obvious to the broad network of problem causes and their relationships. In so doing, it helps define both short term and long term solutions to the problem.

THE 5 WHY PROCESS:
1. Write a statement of the problem on the left side of work surface
2. List all the causes on note cards and place them in a column immediately to the right of the problem statement
3. Make each of these causes, the target of the next level of "why?". Sometimes it should be phrased "why does this situation cause the problem?".
4. Continue to turn each successive "cause" into a new problem statement and ask "why?".
5. Do not stop until you reach a "root cause" such as a policy, procedure, system or training.

Here is an example of a 5 Why addressing a quality problem in a plastics manufacturing plant:

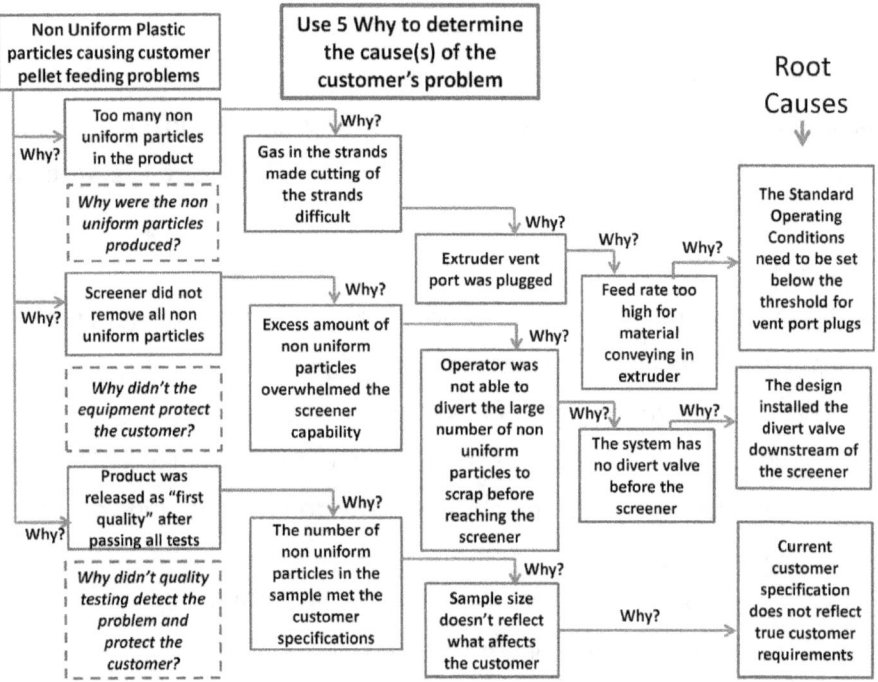

TOOLKIT

Here is an example of the use of 5 Why on an invoicing error:

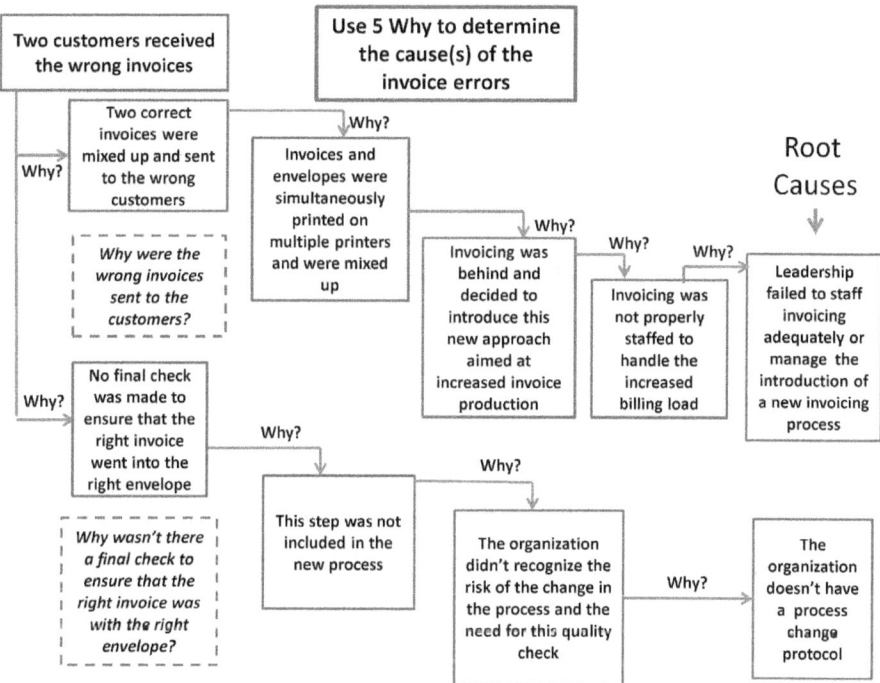

j) Brainstorming:

Brainstorming is a technique used for getting the greatest number of ideas about a given subject. Team members discuss problems and try to come up with probably causes or possible solutions. Quantity of ideas is better than quality in brainstorming. By listing a large number of ideas, it is more likely that the best ideas will be generated.

GUIDELINES:
1. Write down all ideas where everyone can see them
2. Encourage everyone to participate
3. No ideas are criticized..only questions for understanding
4. Challenge the group to "think outside the box"
5. Encourage building on others ideas
6. Use data and facts whenever possible but don't discourage opinion
7. Once all ideas are generated, decide as a team how to converge on which ideas are best to pursue further. This 4 box matrix can be used to make this evaluation:

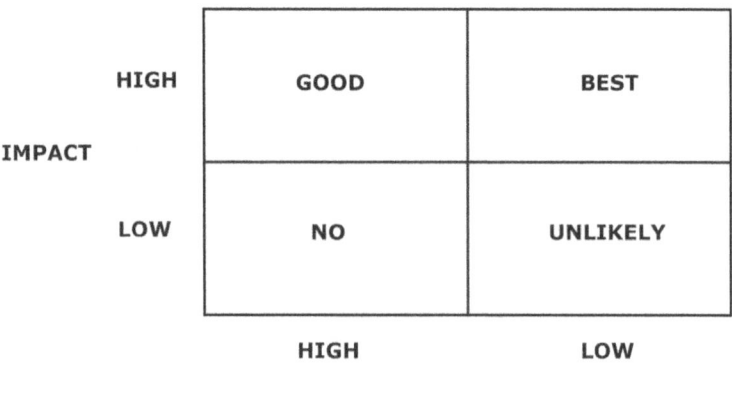

k) Fishbone Diagram:

List all of the possible factors in each category that could impact the problem or provide the desired improvement. After listing ideas at the top level, each factor can then be subdivided into factors that impact that category.

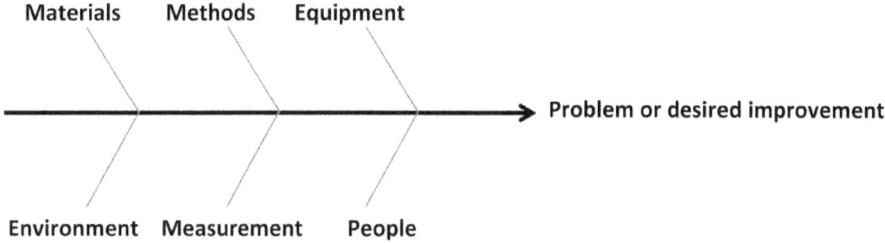

I) Pareto Diagram:

A Pareto diagram is a bar chart in which values are presented in order from largest to smallest. It is typically used to visualize the frequency with which certain problems occur or to visualize the impact of certain problems from highest to lowest. Below is an example showing production downtime losses both in hours (bars) and cumulative percentages (line).

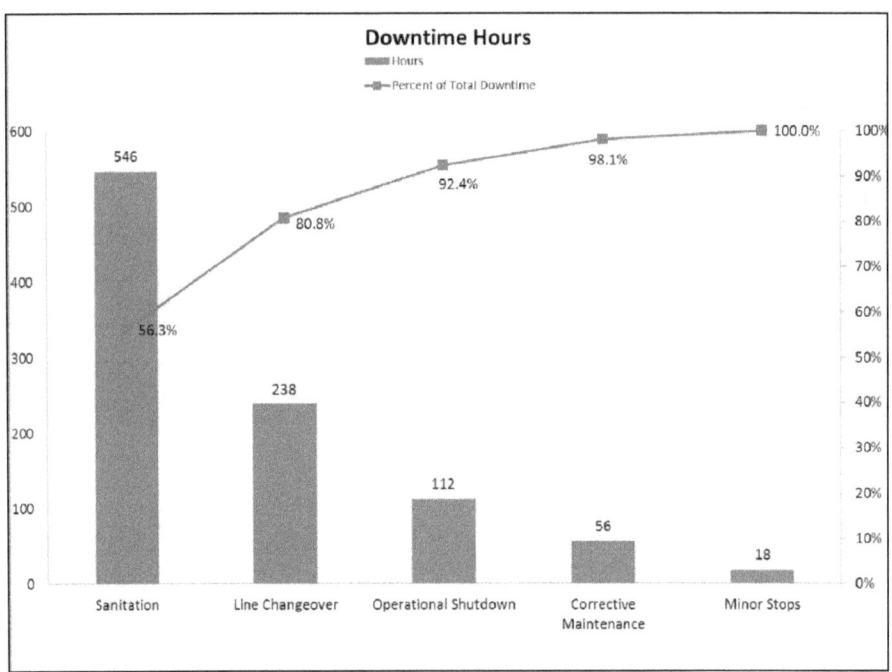

m) Planning a Meeting:

To plan an effective meeting or part of a kaizen event, it can be thought of as a process: inputs, agenda and outputs or products. The first step is to be clear on the purpose of the meeting. Here is a planning model:

Step 1. Why? Why? …What is the purpose the meeting is trying to achieve? The purpose is NOT the results of the meeting but rather the higher purpose or "bigger picture" goal – usually business or customer driven.

Step 2. Define the Inputs, Agenda and Results

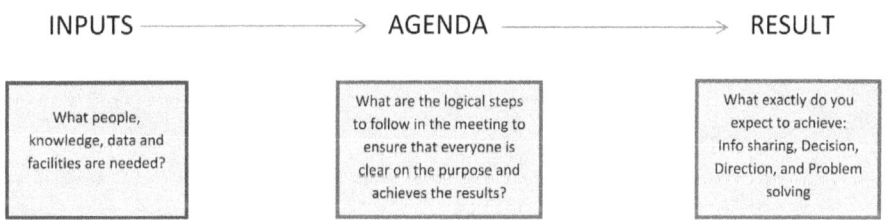

GLOSSARY

Control Plan – A list of specific actions including timing and responsibilities that need to be performed to sustain the changes implemented by the kaizen. Ideally, control plans are incorporated into the organization's Operating Directions

Operating Directions – Comprehensive set of detailed procedures that describe how a process is to be operated.

Punchlist – A list of items that need to be completed before a job is considered complete

Scope Creep – When a project adds new challenges or scope after the project is underway

Six Sigma – A comprehensive improvement process that relies on statistical analysis and a structured project by project approach

Standard Work – A list of specific tasks and timing required for a given job

Test Authorization – A detailed test protocol that specifies how a process or piece of equipment is to be run during an authorized test. Because a Test Authorization can have safety or quality implications, it normally is reviewed before authorization by a broad cross section of the organization before being authorized.

REFERENCES

Liker, Jeffrey K. *The Toyota Way*, New York: McGraw-Hill, 2004.

Mann, David. *Creating a Lean Culture*, New York: Productivity Press, 2005.

MacMillan, et. al. *Kaizen Playbook*, Tempe, Az: AIT Group, 2006.

Scholtes, Peter R. *The Team Handbook*, Madison, Wi: Joiner Associates, 1988.

www.ingramcontent.com/pod-product-compliance
Lightning Source LLC
Chambersburg PA
CBHW071817170526
45167CB00003B/1335